Providence

poems by

Zana Previti

Finishing Line Press
Georgetown, Kentucky

Providence

Copyright © 2017 by Zana Previti
ISBN 978-1-63534-297-0 First Edition
All rights reserved under International and Pan-American Copyright Conventions.
No part of this book may be reproduced in any manner whatsoever without written permission from the publisher, except in the case of brief quotations embodied in critical articles and reviews.

ACKNOWLEDGMENTS

This chapbook was completed during time made possible by the Penn State Altoona Emerging Writer-in-Residence fellowship. The writers Ron Carlson and Michelle Latiolais, and the poets Bob Wrigley, Alexandra Teague, and Ron McFarland, were instrumental in inspiring and supporting this project.

Publisher: Leah Maines

Editor: Christen Kincaid

Cover Art: Doug Kiklowicz

Author Photo: Zana Previti

Cover Design: Elizabeth Maines McCleavy

Printed in the USA on acid-free paper.
Order online: www.finishinglinepress.com
　　　　　also available on amazon.com

Author inquiries and mail orders:
Finishing Line Press
P. O. Box 1626
Georgetown, Kentucky 40324
U. S. A.

Table of Contents

Maine 1
The Minnesota Starvation Experiment 4
Galveston, Texas 10
The Museum of Idaho, Idaho Falls.. 14
California.. 18
Notes 25

For my parents

Maine

> ... for a New Englander, love is the only historically coherent emotion.
>
> Jonathan Morse
> "Some of the Things We Mean When
> We Say 'New England'"

Most stories come back
from this sea are sad
or violent, but every August

I come to swim here. More,
to wade with my baby niece
and nephew together into the easy
waves, where they are scared.

A prayer old whalers used
when the weather arrived: Oh, God—
thy sea is so great, and my boat
so small. Weed-green
water slaps us across the shins;

I can hold the entire existence
of these children in my two arms

and when we walk into this wave,
the tide moves and warms them like
blood. They are frightened.

I lift one onto my hip and the other
closes my hand in his.

We skip over hot sand.

My sister towels her little children
briskly. They cower in the spray
of sunscreen. Bunny-shaped
crackers appear, crumble, are

gone. The water, light and hard
on a row of polished scalpels. I love
this because I remember that ocean,
and because I remember these
children's mother as a small girl

squatting before the fire, watching
wood burn; I remember the scent
of winter hanging ice above
our door. The weapons wielded

by the ocean, gleaming white
blades, salted bludgeons throwing
themselves wide-eyed against the rocks—

but the children are burying
dinosaurs in sand—

weapons their earth
brandishes to protect us,
housed in an armory

where the floors have begun
to sink. I swim in the sea
alone. Something nips my heel,
I swim further out and then stop
to tread suspended there, cold
as ice and just as I remember it,

cold, cold. The immense old
age of the Atlantic—

around my body drift the souls
of glaciers, Ediacara, earliest
reef-builders, lost
boats, beasts harpooned
or flayed or drained—

Oh, time, your waters are so big
and these children are too small
to survive you. The stories back
from this mystery are stories
of boats lost and crushed, fishermen
drowned and drowned again,
vessels of war stalking
the rocky coast, and still

I return here every August
to swim and carry tiny beloveds
into its waving greeting
happy bedlam. My sister

watches her children with her face
a mask of steady, everyday
terror. And still, she releases them

from their dino-bedecked towels
to run clumsily over the sand to the edge
of where swarming life began and still
thrashes against its own diminishing,

to shout my name over the waves'
shouting its devotions to a sea-
god less feared than it deserves, to listen
for my own voice to come back to them

and to wait for someone—
someone they love
because they remember her voice
speaking to them before they were born
to carry them in.

The Minnesota Starvation Experiment

> He believes he is protected by divine Providence, and so do we. But we also believe that we are a part of that divine Providence.
>
> Commandant Mäder,
> Swiss Guard

My grandmother's generation learned
how to split an atom and used
this knowledge unsurprisingly
      Frogmen at that time
would swim long distances underwater
alone and very quietly place
bombs on the hulls of ships then
swim away like dissolving lace

A different kind of swimming
Frogmen also swam with flippers to the shallows
off Normandy Beach   noted
each mine and swam back

while in the Warsaw Ghetto the nurses poisoned
the babies to save them
from Treblinka   The babies were starving
to death   The nurses who had been
their mothers were also starving to death

while in Minnesota pacifists turned their bodies over to
the men trying to prepare for what would come
after it was over
This was the Minnesota Starvation Experiment

These are the days of time travel
We can see the past in photographs
and films   I have watched many films

Nazi-Occupied Warsaw 1941
Food Rations

2,613 kcal/day for Germans
699 kcal/day for Poles
184 kcal/day for Jews

The doctors guessed that for the young healthy Americans
1573 kcal/day could mimic the situation in Europe in 1944

and this was a fair guess
because who would imagine
anything like the truth
who had not seen it

At night   lights from the beach
make triangles of gold polish
on the waters of the Channel
each pointing away

like the tips of gleaming spears
Carve lintels into your ribcage
If you want to help
dig an apse in your lungs
build our church

They could see their bones emerge
Their spines knocked against the backs of chairs
Some did not dream

To lure the remaining Jewish families onto the train
which would take them to Treblinka
the Nazis promised
one piece of bread with marmalade

Stand numbly in line
to be weighed and tested

The doctors are worried and serious
You have become irritable and violent
You have begun to hunch over your portion
of potatoes as if you are hoarding gold
or something even more valuable You still
laugh but not very much and you are quiet

The doctors believe in the end of the war
and the emptying of the camps; those we had
been in time to save
at least bodily

would emerge starving
Someone had to be prepared to do no harm
not to kill them again with food   Someone had
to know what happens to a starving
body and how to bring it back In Warsaw as they
starved the doctors studied their own
starvation and that of their families
And it was groundbreaking research because there were so many
subjects who participated
Someone had to know
what had happened to them
at least bodily   at least bodily

    The doctors have told you about those camps
    and at first you were outraged
    would do anything to help
    but now you are swollen everywhere and hungry
    you lie in your bed except you walk
    two miles to where the food is and back
    because there is food there and you have
    no food

    You dream of wild feasting
    and wake up frantic with
    fear and guilty panic the cold need to purge

You want to help
you said that you wanted to help
you promised
The doctors wake you up in the morning now
to perform the drama
of what they only
guess is happening
inside Dachau, Bergen-Belson,
Treblinka. You said you would do what you could to help
and this is what you have been called to do
Remember you were outraged
You haul rocks,
dig useless holes, drag bags
of sand nowhere. You paint the broad
side of one farmer's barn seventeen times;
sometimes you catch in the wind
the baking scent of bread in the night
You think you can smell the sea
You want to have a hot bath
but that is not allowed

Time is moving   past the now decrepit barn
outside Minneapolis   It is snowing

there now as it was   has   innumerable
hours now gone   Time is moving past
the coast near my home
where storms have made
new graves of old boats

Even in the cold
we begin to be burned
to burn ourselves
these are the generations of guns   standing   loaded
of stopping for death   The generations
in which we begin to patch our heaviest
errors with the bones

of our lakes

This is years ago

my only memory of Minnesota   Dressed like a frogman in black
my sister is surrounded by gray
rocks   She once waded and was pushed back
on the beach in winter And waves break
maliciously   the way to the water is through
wet rocks like the vertebrae of a snake

And the snow continues
She carries a surfboard above her head so that it seems
she plans to dash it onto
the stones   The wind here

cuts delicate slices of the cold and serves them
on ice   What a place to starve in this extreme

of winter   But I am only seven now and do not know My sister looks penned
by her black suit like skin She jumps and is gone
when I blink   I don't know how long to pretend
I will be okay left alone

on this Duluth beach   Is the earth impressed that we try
so hard to stay   These bone

yards of epochs   time   time   I can identify
her feet   kicking   and up on the board This
is when I run along the beach so I am in time
to meet her when she comes in But I miss

her I cannot run like a wave She disappears
and then   is a little black fist

running in the snow toward me   kicking my fear

behind her like a child   happy through a black mask
What cold serious water in Minnesota   We are the only ones here
We watch over the ocean   fast

to the rock and fast to the wave I have nothing to ask

Years and years
So much research and many participants   A friend returned from
Phnom Penh
                              There are ghosts bleeding
in the road   These stones are the generations
upon which we build   images of the end of us

In films we crumble like wheat We do not survive
our massacres   We tell stories of monsters
generations of fallen superheroes and failed
holy men   Time is moving past

coral reefs now bleeding from their sides
into chalices of seagrass

In water frogmen placed bombs and submarines
waited to do the same
and also I learned to swim
There is nothing understandable about
history except love is the only coherent emotion Everything
else is a waste of resources

To starve to death requires
only time and nothing   I am
you are   we are trying to survive and only time
reminds us that we cannot   I can make with my body
a transept if I lie
down here   with you

Galveston, Texas

> 'I will lift up mine eyes unto the hills, from whence cometh my help,' had been another charm against trouble; though I have since learned that the last five words of the original Hebrew are really a question, not a relative clause.
>
> Robert Graves
Goodbye to All That

Also fear is a historically coherent emotion; Galveston was hugely unprepared for the hurricane.
Since I have been young, I have loved to bring mystery novels into the bathtub and read them. The eyewall lifts gulfs as a film demon conjures the dead. In the bathtub I would read
detective novels only: intelligent
British stabbings, snowbound
mannered revenge, jewels gone
vanished.

In Galveston, September 1900, suddenly families
like baby turtles scuttering in the streets. In my favorites
the secret is so dense and hidden
even the slim cool detective cannot
believe it. Not *him?*! In very old
photographs the houses
lilt as if unsure. The houses, asleep
at the table, lean too much on their
elbows and topple. Ideally
I like a cheap paperback. It
will get damp in the bath. There is not a single person
left alive who saw the 1900 Galveston Hurricane; but
there are turtles to whom that storm is recent history. Mysteries form best around
a cloud of aggressively strange characters, or those ill with their secrets.

That hurricane was so strong
and bad that it kept climbing up
north and it killed some fishermen

all the way in Nova Scotia. I loved
the bath so much that for my seventh
birthday my parents let me stay
in it as long as I liked, until the water
was very cold and they worried. On the list of casualties is

MACKEY (Mrs. W.G.),
MACKEY (child of W.G.)(1),
MACKEY (child of W.G.)(2),
MACKEY (child of W.G.)(3),
MACKEY (child of W.G.)(4)
but W.G. Mackey is not on the list.

I read that the word *massacre* is derived from the Latin
for *butcher shop*. Perhaps W.G. had died already. Initially
I found this thought consoling. The detectives usually know the victim, or at least
they've seen that body somewhere before. Was she the heiress in the
newspaper? American Heritage ranked it first
in Our Top Ten Greatest Natural Disasters. Antecedent of *our*? I heard some men
drowned in trenches in WWI; this may be false. The proliferation of corpses
was such that 700 were loaded onto carts and wheeled away, to be dumped
into the sea. The work of carrying each body, one by one, and lifting them onto
the boat, and then pushing them into the water, this work was done only by the
black male population of Galveston because the group of white
men who had tried collapsed and became too sick
to do the work. My father read a book to me once, in which
a peach grows to incredible size and floats across the ocean.

I visited Texas three times and did not care for it. These detectives—
spinsters or Chief Inspectors—remember at last the vital thing, place
it inside the empty space, a porcelain swan in the glass cabinet. They always
do. When they arrived they must have gasped at that sea, the gulf spread out,

glinting as though newly hatchet-split, glinting like a new hatchet, and sharp just
for them. In the bathtub, sounds are muffled. I live alone but I close the door.

The youngest,
I would be
(child of J.J.)(3)

And there is nothing
to explain why   I am reading how
the body came to lie in the library
and why the Mackey children
drowned. I avoid this
topic like water-
borne disease. I have secrets
but not one I would kill for—
What secret has a storm?

There is a pleasure in not knowing; but only insofar that Knowing is slouching toward us, soon, in a hundred pages. We can prepare ourselves for tragedy, surprise,
but I am worried, half-asleep in night, that we like Galveston have underestimated, that we have not prepared well enough. Damp pages of murders line my heart. In poetry, each line makes no sense to me. I dislike most of what I read and see.

Galveston was hugely unprepared for that hurricane. The legs of the houses crumpled and gave out under them. Outrun.
At mass they said "mystery of faith" and I got excited, but it didn't mean what I thought.

"the corpses could no longer be
moved, except in fragments."   The priest would say *We lift up our hearts* and we would reply *We lift them up to the Lord*. I imagined holding a drippy heart muscle toward the sky.

They set fire to what was left in the street. Because
of course no one has made any sense of death yet.
The bodies they buried at sea washed up again
on the beach; they burned those in piles in great
beach bonfires. In the parlor, company assembled, the detective says,
Here is why she died. Or: Here is he who killed him. I am
safe in the bathtub and everything is logical. Lazy
fingers of steam on my neck.

On his infallibility:
"when the dogma was read out the Pope said, 'Is that all right, gents?' All the gents said 'Placet' but two said 'Non placet.' But the Pope: "You be damned! Kissmearse! I'm infallible!'"

Newspapers made sure the public knew what the white men
were doing to help versus what the black men were doing. Puzzlingly.
Someone is in control,
my detectives assure me. There is a design
in all of this. Largely the houses of the outskirted poor protected the houses
of the downtown fancy. We are all a clever story. Enjoy that bath. We fear
what we remember:
primitive enemies, animals that can best us. Before there was light, God
was hovering over the waters. So God remembers waters, huh.

They dunked me when I was born.
So they clung together and trudged,
if they'd lived, over the drowned dogs
and were grateful. And here I am like a child
playing in the water, reading stories
of death and so happy
and warm. Non placet, non placet,
non placet.

The Museum of Idaho, Idaho Falls

> Their monument sticks like a fishbone
> in the city's throat.
>
> >Robert Lowell
> >"For the Union Dead"

Much later, I learn what's been done
in a church. It'll be on the news.
A field trip swarms the room and hums
across the exhibit, and   one
small girl is worried. No fission
lesson soothes; she moves as though to
search. What awful thing has been done
inside the church? It will be on the news.

One boy draws an apocalypse
on his arm, blue mad pen frontier
on skin. Violent museum, this:
model bombs, airships on airstrips.
I'm watching the girl, who seems sick
with worry, search the reactor
for something she's misplaced, or missed.
What's been lost? What has disappeared?

Like all museums, this one is neat and tidy.
I've been in others . . . old places, former prisons
or palaces that keep the past upright, glass-eyed,
polished like all history. In Italy, caught mid-stride,
a marble woman runs; her hands dissolve into five
fingers of flowers. Cross country, in Charleston,
a small museum cleans for special art, tidies
itself for a martyr trapped in his travelling prison—

a painting, the size of a brownie tin,
depicting the saint Bartholomew's torture.
With a currycomb, a man scrapes away skin
and the tissue is soft pink within—

the torturer must go deeper
to reach bone. Does he not want to bleed him
further? Maybe, a good man, he cannot
subject a good man to this torture.

Or perhaps he is only following orders,
righteously, dutifully. Maybe he aches to prolong
it; maybe the task brings him some joy or comfort
he needs badly. Those days were colder
than mine. Skinning a man alive may have cured
some icy thing in him, and his curing act belongs
under glass and guard. He is only following orders,
knowing it is not right but going along, going along.

The voices of this field trip have overrun
my thought. Some of the past is only a story.
The boy with the scribbled arm has begun
to help his panicked classmate. They run
from the Bikini Islands to the cold-hearted sun
of Los Alamos; they search the reactor on all fours.
I want to ask what they are looking for. They run
to each other with nothing. I want to know the story.

She cries. We know it has been lost
forever. I, for someone who
cannot see what's gone, feel this loss
too strongly, yearn to own all lost
and vanished stories: Chaos,
for which we split the atom, knew
the face of need and scent of cost.
The children leave. I watch them go.

I watch a mounted screen when the children are gone:
Lise Meitner smokes and looks me right in the eye;
uranium blossoms, spirals, unsheathes on the screen.
I watch the collisions. I watch energy release until it is gone:

like the snake of us shedding its skin, and slithering on.
I remember the story of a rabbi who was skinned alive
and yet prayed calmly throughout. Or, no—it was a monk,
in Tuol Sleng. No one can make order here. Neither can I.

When I leave the museum, I am a little frantic,
weirdly fey. It rains and I feel like a desperate King Lear,
who would beat his Fool for unruly, loud and manic
speech. But for silence too. Yet the Fool never left—panicked
with cold and fear and perhaps knowing how it
would all end, a death no one would ever see. And yet he risked
all that, his life and what was left of his happy antics,
his weird rhyming joy. It rains, it is raining, my dearest King Lear.

On the news tomorrow a pastor will comment
on what has happened to many confusions
sitting in rows. "The perpetrator has been caught,"
he will assure his parish tomorrow. He'll go on: "But
the killer remains at large." And we will all know what
he means. We know, have seen, what the past becomes.
On the news, pastors and pundits will comment
on what has happened today. Just confusion.

Cordelia knew what she was risking when she said
Nothing. But I think even if she did not,
her sisters did, and tried to keep that anger
from her. They took it, but inside themselves.
Lately I think there has been a massacre
every day. No, not just lately. And lately
there are days when I look down to see
if it is my hand holding the weapon.

Sometimes it is my hand holding the weapon.
Sometimes I let it clatter to the street. I run
away before they see me.
Somewhere there is a Lear who loves his children,

all of them, even the angry and covetous animal-
like children, even the fools, even the liars

even the murderers, even those who do not pluck
out anyone's eyes but watch sedately as another
hand reaches and maims calmly, calmly. Even those

children. Even the bad ones. Somewhere a King
Lear loves even these and if he is wandering in the storm
as I am now,
it is raining, it is raining—
If he wanders in a storm he will have his band of help
and when he dies, they will write him down. In the rain
in the street,   I am holding the currycomb. I have
nightmares.   I can see their skins quivering and still
on my lap.   I drop it.   I drop my weapon

I wish to drop my weapon
My arms are become flayers' rakes
I wish to drop my weapon   My body is so sharp

so I file   file   file the edges down

at night   but I have become so sharp
 the world is all   a whetstone
If I turn to the past my body becomes so razor keen
and when I turn back   the smell of a   skin

and something bleeding   and I have done it myself
  I am looking down at my hands

California

> Ten masts at each make not the altitude
> Which thou hast perpendicularly fell;
> Thy life's a miracle. Speak yet again.
> > William Shakespeare
> > *King Lear* Act IV, Scene vi

I didn't have time to write a short poem so I wrote a long one instead.
> The past has not gone away;
> you wade further into time
> and it into you. It becomes
> you: water in a teapot,
> it becomes the teapot.
> "It is not a daily increase," said Bruce Lee.
> "It's a daily decrease. Hack away."

It is, as they've said, a fairly golden
state. I have led myself here. I live
here by the sea for all of my mornings.
No one knows me,

so the television keeps the lamps
lit; one channel plays only
dubbed Kung Fu films, many
I have never seen.

I imagine bodies arriving here
and clearing space for themselves
with their weapons, mapping

the new coast, building white
missions with tanning vats for hides
and square cemeteries. Bruce Lee
was born in San Francisco;
he would teach his son Gong
Fu in their living room: the baby
barefoot and serious, the father
barefoot and serious. So faced,

they would make their way, one
move, another, across the carpet,
one big and his tiny copy.
The poor are plundered and are dead,
did eat manna and are dead.

     My father read a book to me, once, in which a young boy is orphaned and abused. A peach grows to incredible size and, broken from its tree, rolls off and quickly through the country, finally to splash off from the White Cliffs of Dover, and fall into the sea. The child along with it.

I have led myself this whole
long way. I live here by the sea
for all of my mornings. Through my window
I hear waves foaming and bullying
the shore. No one knows me.

In this scene a fat white man
puts up his dukes. Bruce Lee
is slim and in the corner—
he is nearly outside the shot.
In a moment he will move
across the screen like a dragon
whipping his tail and I will pause
in what I am doing, carrying some
box to the living room, stand
and watch until he has finished.

I imagine seeing something
as someone must have seen
something, for the very first time—

maybe a man, but maybe a wagon,
maybe the remnant of a strange-
smelling fire—and watching the same
tide go in and come out again. Go west

to escape, my friend.

In this house by the beach I am tidy.
I tuck the corners of the bedsheet.
Do you remember your childhood?
From my front door, the view
of the old air force base looms,
the highway looms, like the walls
of a wrecked city.

Going there,
nearly there.

Oh, the Americans
in this film! We end
ourselves unabashed.

I dream my back and arms are the ribs
holding the wagon's cover of fretted
gold and these oxen will die
pretty soon. In the rain,
I live here by the sea for all of
my mornings. Through my window
I can hear the tuning sounds of a new
ocean. No one knows me.

How awful goodness was, and how in shape
   so lovely. My verse is dumb
and blank. You are all a mystery.

Pho Viet Harbor makes
my dinner almost every night.
Thao brings me noodles; she smokes
secret cigarettes outside, behind
the parking, tilts her head
back and blows the smoke
into the sky. This far north, more trees

than I pictured when I planned. I put too much
salt on everything. At the window
I can just make out a face
I think we know. We are
jostling in our wagon
train; we are crowding;
we can hear the water now;
nearly there
we are nearly there.

      Hector, before he ran into battle, kissed his wife and baby son goodbye. The child saw Hector in his armor and cried, afraid. And so Hector laughing lifted and took the helmet from his head and lay it gleaming on the ground, showed his son his face, adored and kissed him goodbye.

Across the country, the seaweed bewilders
a green Atlantic. My sisters' voices spoke
to me before I was born: I remember
them. On this coast, the water is warm
as a bath. And everyone travels so far
to be happy, and everyone travels out
as far as they go. Fighting in the Trojan
dark and mist Ajax finally,
maddened by all that brutality soaking
the sand of the beach, calls to his god
      Kill us if you will
      but kill us in the light.

     And here the light comes down even in the forest
     and here you can even be alone
     and here there are days like fresh grasses
     grasslands which end eventually
     at a beach or war.

When Ajax and the Greeks defeated the Trojans, they threw Hector's baby from the walls of the city. In a Roman museum sits an antique vase in which the Greeks kill King Priam by beating him to death with the body of his grandson. Non
placet.

I live far from home and I do not want
to return. I am perpetually afraid.
I was always a gluttonous sleeper;
I sleep like a baby here. The screen
door, always open, the window always
open, the rain coming in and dousing
my blanket. There is no further
west to go; here is the end. The walls of
graffiti promise something
I cannot read
in bright colors. Somewhere has happened the worst
and the bodies cannot be moved but in fragments;
I dream. I wake up frantic
in guilt, guilty panic and fear,
from whence comes my help.

"I am a very foolish fond old man," says Lear. "I am doubtful," he says.

My child, Cordelia,
so I am, I am.

It is the very end of the play. If I could I would lay
it all gleaming on the ground, all of it. Off, you
lendings. I wish to drop my weapons now. Off, helmet,
off off off.

Gloucester's eyes are gone and he is wandering. A madman takes his arm.

Do you know the way to the Dover cliffs, Gloucester asks the madman. The madman is naked.
I do, the madman says. I know the way.
Take me there, asks Gloucester, to the edge of a high cliff like a bowed head.

Then you may leave me. I will know the way from there.
        The mad man takes his arm and leads his father to the sea.

I can hold my entire existence
in one slipper of skin

and when I drive across the bay
the bridge bends and sways as one wooded country,
Arden or Birnam wold crawling with stories:
tragedies, mysteries, comedies, fantastic
tales, gospels: a stranger arriving
or a traveler, embarking. Across
the bridge, scrawled on the wall by a refugee
passing through, perhaps from Vietnam,
Cambodia, perhaps Laos or a place
I have never been and never will go,
   at the former now abandoned
     and slowly graying Hamilton Air Force Base,
        graffito in slanting letters:

Your father has been waiting   for you forever
your life is a miracle

Notes

"Maine"

The epigraph for this section, by Jonathan Morse, appeared in the article "Some of the Things We Mean When We Say 'New England,'" published in *The Emily Dickinson Journal* in 1996.

The prayer, "Oh, God – thy sea is so great, and my boat so small," is one famously adorning the Seamen's Bethel in New Bedford, Massachusetts.

"The Minnesota Starvation Experiment"

The epigraph for this poem was found in the book *The Pope's Army: 500 Years of the Papal Swiss Guard*, by Robert Royal.

The raw information and historical facts for this section came from a variety of sources. The book *Hunger: An Unnatural History,* by Sharman A. Russell, provided details on the Warsaw ghetto rationing, and the starvation research conducted there at that time. It also contained a helpful chapter on the Minnesota Experiment. Another helpful source was the article "They Starved So That Others Be Better Fed: Remembering Ancel Keys and the Minnesota Experiment," by Leah Kalm and Richard Semba, and published in the *Journal of Nutrition* in 2005.

Frogmen, the forebears of today's Navy SEALS, emerged in Italy in World War II, and their use became clear to the Americans, who began to train their soldiers in a similar way.

This section also borrows language from two Emily Dickinson poems, "My Life Had Stood a Loaded Gun," and "Because I could not Stop for Death."

"Galveston, Texas"

Much of the information on the Galveston Hurricane was culled from Gary Cartwright's history of the city, *Galveston: A History of the Island*.

The quote: "the corpses could no longer be moved, except in fragments" comes from an October 1900 article in *National Magazine*, written by Clarence Ousley. "Thrilling Experiences in the Galveston Storm" details Ousley's personal experience and survival of the storm and describes the initial phases of recovery.

The record of the Mackey family was found at the Galveston and Texas History Center, Rosenberg Library website, which lists the official

list of casualties from the storm.
They report that over "8,000 people in Galveston city and county lost their lives in the 1900 Storm. At the time of the Storm identification of every victim proved impossible."

This poem also references the book *James and the Giant Peach*, by Roald Dahl, the poem "The Second Coming," by W.B. Yeats, and the first chapter, second verse of Genesis.

The quoted story recounting the Vatican Council of 1870, which declared the Pope's infallibility, comes from a November 13, 1906 letter from James Joyce to his brother Stanislaus. Walton Litz and Robert Scholes included the excerpt in their edited critical edition of Joyce's *Dubliners*.

"The Museum of Idaho, Idaho Falls"

This section begins with an allusion to the June 2015 mass shooting at the Emanuel African Methodist Episcopal Church, in which nine were killed. Some of the victims' families publicly forgave the killer. I quote Rev. Dr. William Barber III who, in reaction to this shooting, wrote that "Their forgiveness is also an act of resistance to the attempts to lay the blame for this horror at the feet of one man. If America is serious about this moment, we cannot just cry ceremonial tears while at the same time refusing to support the martyred Reverend and his parishioners' stalwart fight against the racism that gave birth to the crime. The perpetrator has been caught, but the killers are still at large: the deep wells of American racism and white supremacy from which Dylann Roof drank."

Allusions throughout the poem include: the 1644 painting "The Martyrdom of Saint Bartholomew," by Josepe de Ribera, or "Lo Spagnoletto," Bernini's marble "Daphne and Apollo," and Shakespeare's *King Lear* and *Romeo and Juliet*.

This section of the poem was influenced by Robert Lowell's "For the Union Dead" and Katy Didden's "At Chartres."

Lise Meitner, an Austrian-born Jew, studied with Max Planck in the early half of the 20th century. Though she later converted to Christianity, she was forced to emigrate after the 1938 Anschluss. She collaborated with Otto Hanh, and together they discovered the process of nuclear fission. Only Hahn was awarded the Nobel Prize in Chemistry.

The article "Buddhism in a Dark Age," by Ian Harris, and *For the Time Being*, by Annie Dillard, provided the details of the Khmer Rouge's widespread torture of Buddhist monks, and Rabbi Akiva's torture by flaying, respectively.

The closing of this section is partially inspired by Chana Bloch's poem "Goodbye."

"California"

The poem begins with an allusion to Mark Twain: "I didn't have the time to write a short letter, so I wrote a long one instead."

In Season 1, episode 1 of the 1971 television series *Longstreet*, Bruce Lee (as Li Tsung) advises the blind Mike Longstreet to emulate water; the speech became iconic for Lee, and its meaning echoed in many of his interviews and writings.

Apocryphally attributed to Lee: "In building a statue, a sculptor doesn't keep adding clay to his subject. Actually, he keeps chiseling away at the inessentials until the truth of its creation is revealed without obstructions. Thus, contrary to other styles, being wise in Jeet Kune-Do doesn't mean adding more; it means to minimize, in other words to hack away the unessential." Often, this is paraphrased or quoted as "It is not daily increase but daily decrease; hack away the unessential."

A couplet early in the section combines two Biblical verses: "Your fathers ate the manna in the wilderness, and they died" (John 6:49) and "'Because the poor are plundered, because the needy groan, I will now arise,' says the LORD; 'I will place him in the safety for which he longs'" (Psalms 12:5).

This section also contains references to *James and the Giant Peach*, multiple scenes from *King Lear*, *Macbeth*, the *Iliad*, and the Bruce Lee film *The Way of the Dragon*.

A repeated line, with a few variations, is inspired by Frank O'Hara's "Poem Read at Joan Mitchell's," in which he writes "you will live half the year in a house by the sea and half the year in a house in our arms."

. A stanza midway through the poem manipulates a portion of John Milton's *Paradise Lost*. Book IV, lines 844-847: "Abashed the Devil stood, / and felt how awful goodness is, and saw / Virtue in her shape how lovely; saw, and pined / His loss." The lines also figure prominently in the film *The Crow*, in which Bruce Lee's son Brandon starred and, while shooting it, died tragically in an accident.

Hamilton Air Force Base, in Novato California, was used as a processing station for South Asian refugees during and after the Vietnam War. It did, at one time, bear the graffito "your father has been waiting for you forever," though it may now be erased.

Zana Previti was born and raised in New England.

She was educated at Wellesley College, in Wellesley, Massachusetts, where she earned her degree in English; later, she taught high school English at private schools along the East Coast. She earned her MFA in fiction from the University of California, Irvine in 2012, and her MFA in poetry from the University of Idaho in 2016.

Her work has been published in *The New England Review, Hayden's Ferry Review, The Los Angeles Review, Ninth Letter,* and elsewhere. *Tin House* named her a Summer Conference Fiction Scholar in 2014, and her short fiction has been featured on Oregon Public Radio's *State of Wonder.* In 2016, her first play, *The Gorgon,* was performed in a staged reading at the University of Idaho. Zana was recently named the recipient of Poetry International's 2014 C.P. Cavafy Prize for Poetry, and the Fall 2016 Emerging Writer-in-Residence at Penn State Altoona.

Her first novel, *The Chilling Simple,* is forthcoming in 2018 from the University of West Alabama's Livingston Press.

www.ingramcontent.com/pod-product-compliance
Lightning Source LLC
LaVergne TN
LVHW041513070426
835507LV00012B/1534